MW01437704

FIRES AND RADIATORS

Joy Richardson

Illustrated by
Sue Barclay and Dee McLean

Evans Brothers Limited

The author and publishers would like to thank Robert Gwynne B.Sc. for his help and advice in the preparation of this book.

Published by Evans Brothers Limited
2A Portman Mansions
Chiltern Street
London W1M 1LE

First published in Great Britain in 1988 by
Hamish Hamilton Children's Books

© Joy Richardson (text) 1988
© Sue Barclay (illustrations) and Dee McLean (activities)

Designed by Monica Chia

Reprinted 1991

All Rights Reserved. No part of this publication may be reproduced, stored in a retrieval, system, or transmitted, in any form or by any means, electronic, mechanical, photocopying, recording or otherwise, without prior permission of Evans Brothers Limited.

ISBN: 0 237 60243 1

Printed in Spain by GRAFO, S.A.-Bilbao

«Science Seekers» can be used to support your children's work in the National Curriculum.

The ability to relate science to everyday life is described in the programme of study for Key Stages 1 and 2 as an essential element of early science experience. «Children should use a variety of domestic and environmental contexts as starting points for learning science.»

Each book in this series can be related to one Science Attainment Target as follows:

«Down the Plughole»: Attainment Target 5 - Human Influences on the Earth.

«Turn on a Tap»: Attainment Target 9 - Earth and Atmosphere.

«Switch on a Light»: Attainment Target 11 - Electricity and Magnetism.

«Fires and Radiators»: Attainment Target 13 - Energy.

CONTENTS

Cold weather	6
Ways of heating a room	7
Open fires	8–10
Gas fires	11
Electric fires	12–13
Storage heaters	14–15
Central heating boiler	16–17
Central heating pipes	18–20
Central heating pump	21
Central heating radiators	22–27
Temperature control	28
Insulation	29–30
Warm weather	31
Index	32

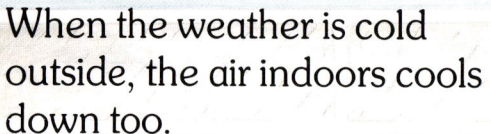

When the weather is cold outside, the air indoors cools down too.

You cannot see whether the air is cold or warm but you can feel the difference.

Heating warms the air in the room and keeps you feeling comfortable.

If the air is too cold it makes you feel shivery.

Heating Chart

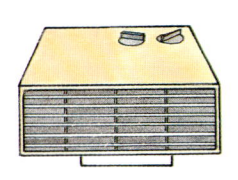

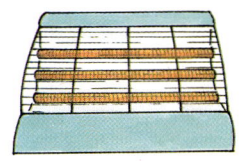

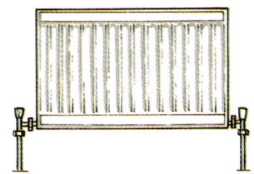

1. There are many different ways of heating a room.

2. Make a chart of rooms in the building. Look round each room to find out how it is heated.

3. On your chart draw all the fires or heaters or radiators you can see.

4. How does each one makes its heat? Does it use coal, or wood, or gas, or oil, or electricity?

5. Never play with the fires and radiators in your house. THEY CAN BE DANGEROUS.

Open fires make heat from coal or wood. Smoke escapes up the chimney. Ashes are left behind in the grate.

Oxygen from the air is needed to make the fire burn.

When a fire is burning, you may feel a draught as air is sucked towards the fire.

Some fires can draw in air from outside through an underfloor pipe. The extra oxygen makes the fire flare up and burn brightly.

Air for Burning

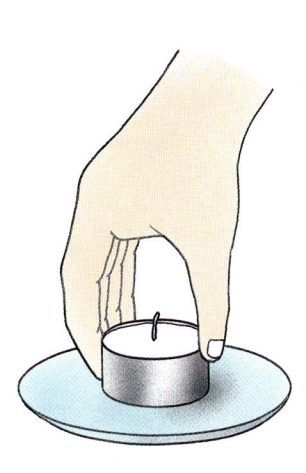

1. Put a night-light candle on a saucer.

2. Light the candle and put a jam jar over it.

3. Watch the flame until it goes out.

4. Try again. This time, whenever the flame begins to die down, lift the jam jar to let in more air.

Can you make the flame burn brightly again?

The candle is like a fire. It needs oxygen to keep it burning.

As a fire burns it gives out energy.

The heat energy from the fire travels out into the room like rays from the sun.

You soon feel hot if you sit close by.

If you hold a book up between you and the fire, the book will block off the heat rays like a cloud covering the sun.

Gas is another fuel which can be burned to make heat.

There is a gas pipe to this fire. When the fire is lit, the gas bursts into flames.

The flames heat up the white clay at the back of the fire. The clay grows hot and gives out heat. This makes the fire feel hotter.

Many heaters run on electricity. Electricity makes heat without flames.

Each bar of this electric fire is made of a coil of wire. When electricity pushes through it, the wire heats up and begins to glow.

There is shiny metal behind the bars. It reflects the heat in the same way that a shiny mirror reflects the light.

Heat rays bounce off the shiny metal. They bounce back into the room.

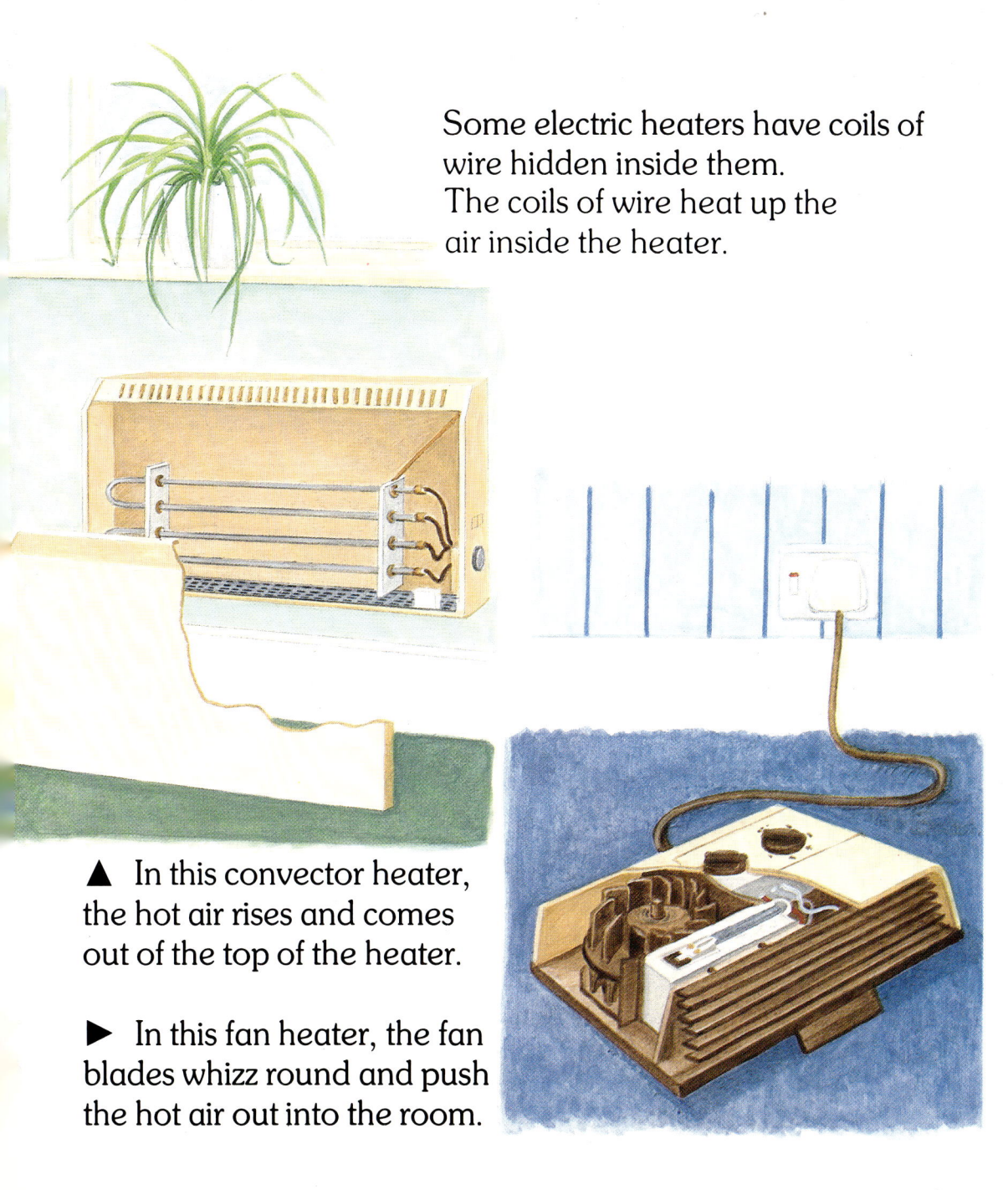

Some electric heaters have coils of wire hidden inside them.
The coils of wire heat up the air inside the heater.

▲ In this convector heater, the hot air rises and comes out of the top of the heater.

▶ In this fan heater, the fan blades whizz round and push the hot air out into the room.

13

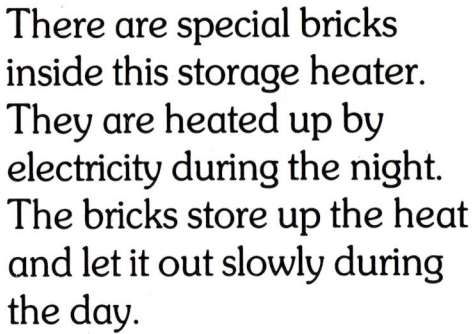

There are special bricks inside this storage heater. They are heated up by electricity during the night. The bricks store up the heat and let it out slowly during the day.

Electricity costs less at night-time, so storage heaters save money.

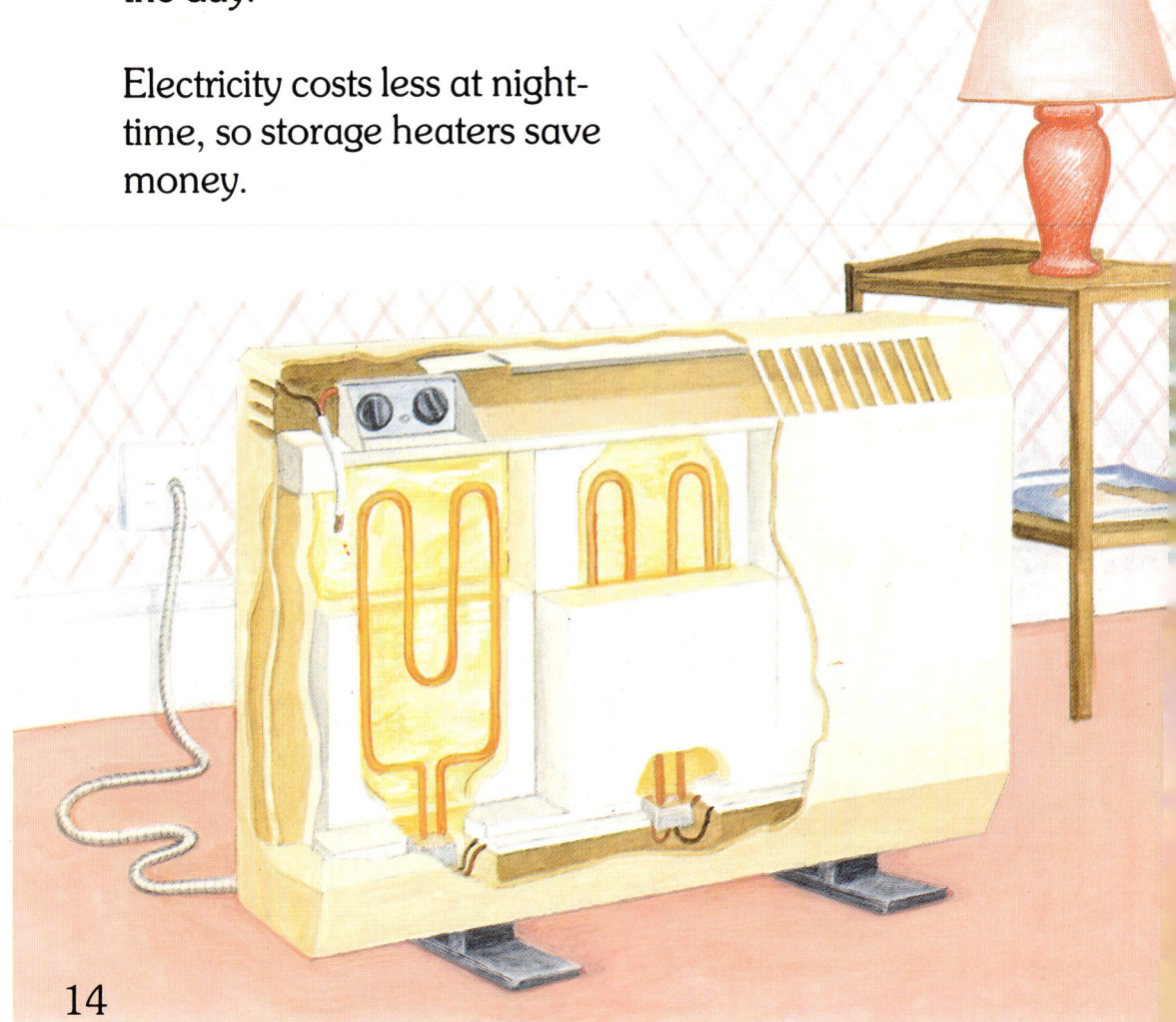

Storing Heat

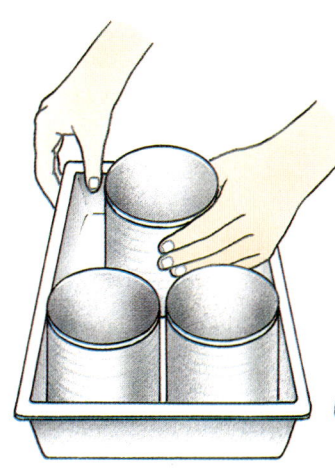

1. Stand three empty tins on a metal baking tray.

2. Half fill one tin with clean dry sand. Put a potato into the second tin. Leave the third tin empty.

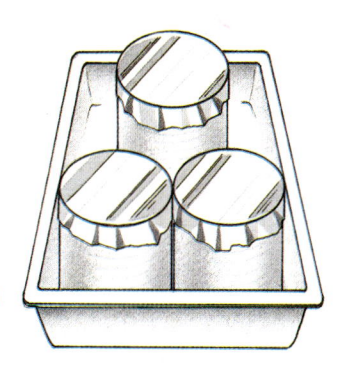

3. Cover the tops with aluminium foil.

4. Pierce a few holes in the foil.

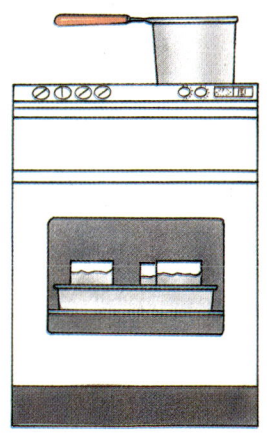

5. With an adult's help, heat the tins in a medium oven for twenty minutes and then take them out.

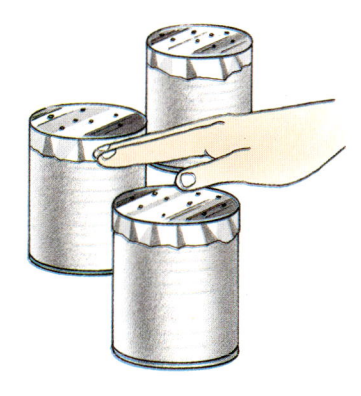

6. Hold your hands close to the tins without touching them. Feel the heat they give out.

Time how long each tin goes on giving out heat. Which is the best storage heater?

Central heating uses one boiler to heat up all the rooms.

The boiler burns fuel such as coal, gas or oil to make a fire. The fire burns inside a strong metal casing.

In gas and oil boilers, a small flame called the pilot light stays alight all the time. You can see it through a little glass window inside the boiler. When the boiler switches on, the pilot light sets the gas or oil alight.

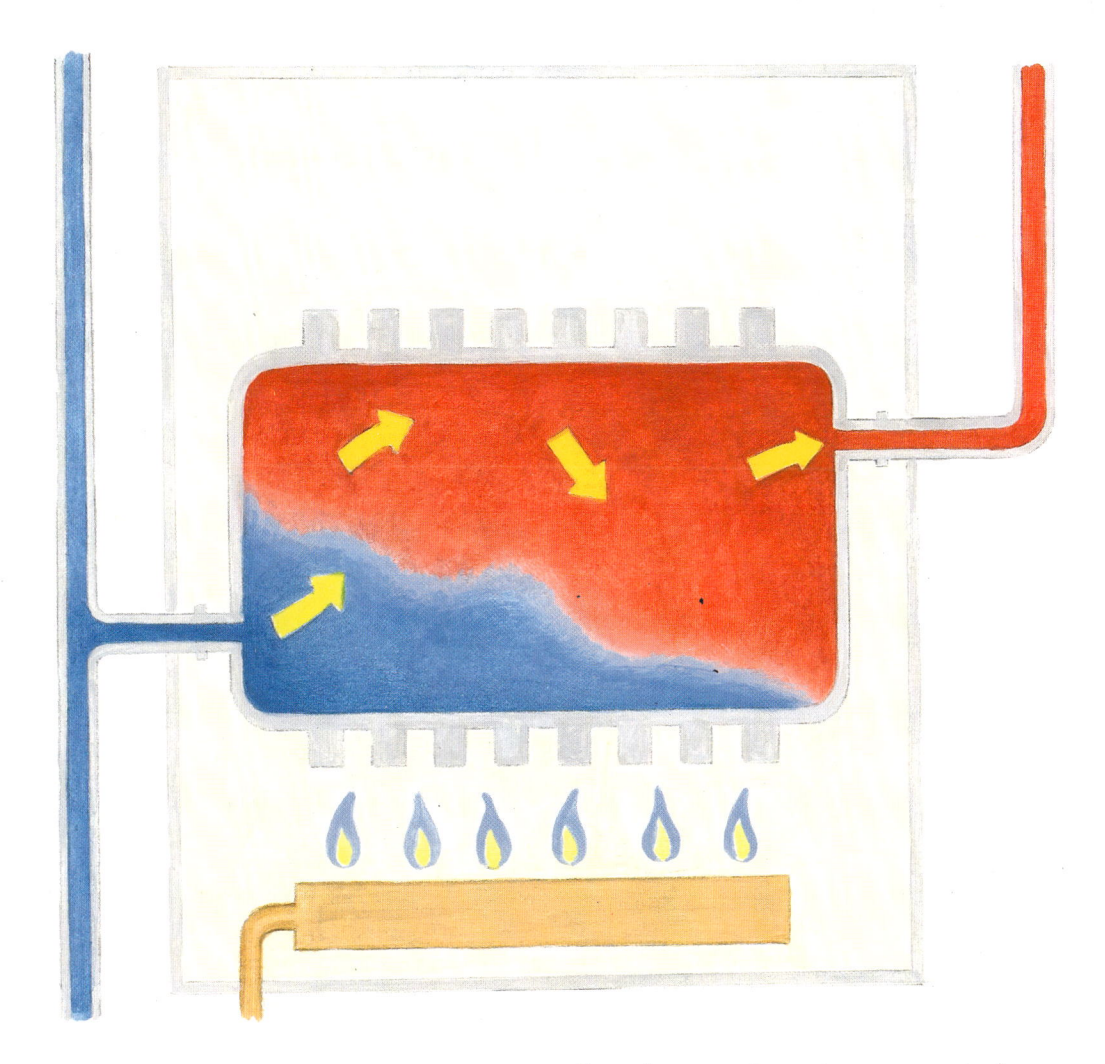

Cold water comes down from a storage tank in the roof.

The water comes down through a pipe into the boiler.

It is heated up in a special metal water box inside the boiler.

The fire in the boiler heats up the metal and makes the water very hot.

17

Pipes from the boiler branch off to each radiator in the house. The pipes are laid in pairs. One pipe carries hot water to the radiator. The other pipe carries used water back to the boiler to be heated up again.

The same water can be used again and again. It is kept topped up by water from the tank.

Water expands as it heats up. It takes up more space. If there is not enough room in the pipes, the extra water can escape up an expansion pipe back into the tank.

19

Pipe Routes

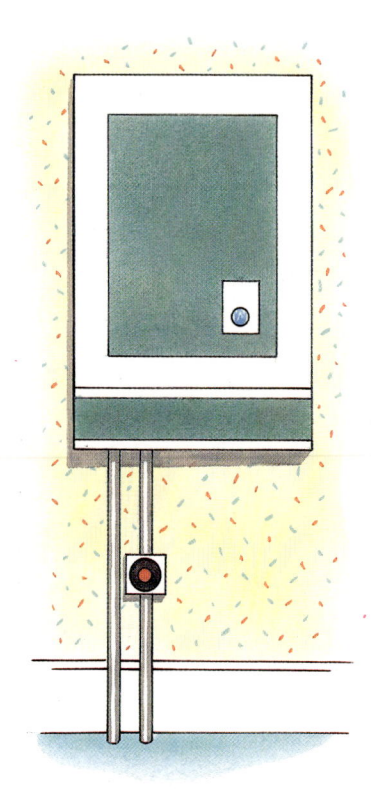

1. Look where the pipes from the boiler go. Then look where the pipes come from into a radiator.

2. Most of the pipework is hidden inside walls and under floors. Can you work out where the pipes go between the boiler and the radiator?

3. Compare the pipe sizes. Has the boiler pipe branched off into smaller pipes?

Water needs pumping to help it up and along the pipes.

The boiler has a pump which is run by electricity. You can hear the pump working when the boiler is on.

The pump is like a water wheel. It spins round fast and pushes the water through the pipes.

The pump keeps water moving through the boiler and out to all the radiators.

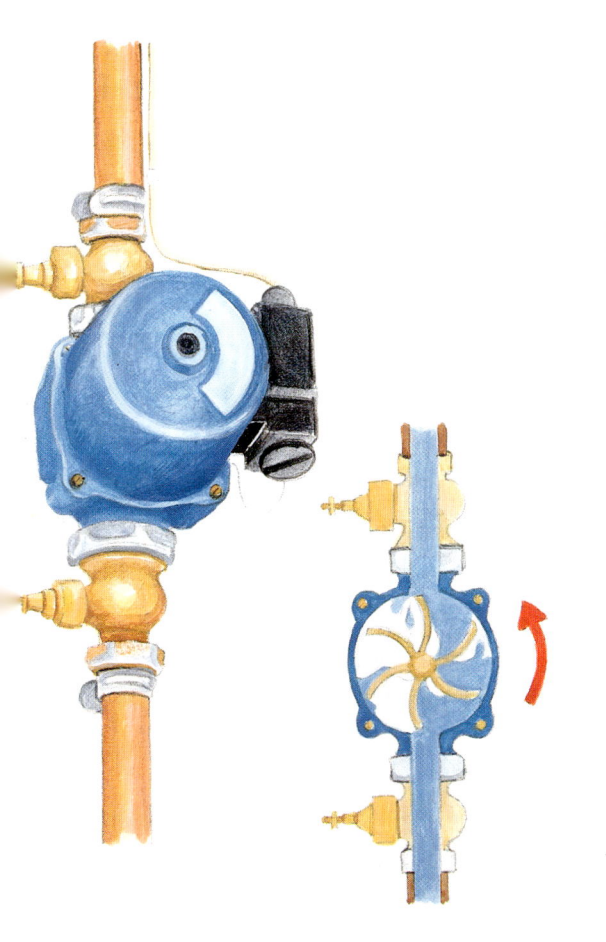

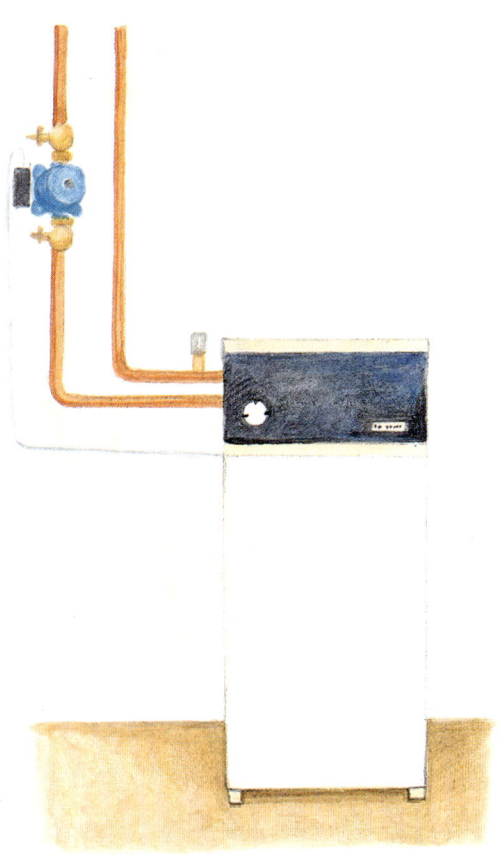

Look at a radiator to find the hollow spaces which fill up with water. Radiators are shaped so that a little hot water heats a lot of metal.

There is a valve on each end of the radiator. One turns on like a tap to let the hot water in.

Hot water fills the space inside the radiator. It pushes old water out through a pipe at the bottom.

When you turn a radiator off, the water stops moving. It soon cools down.

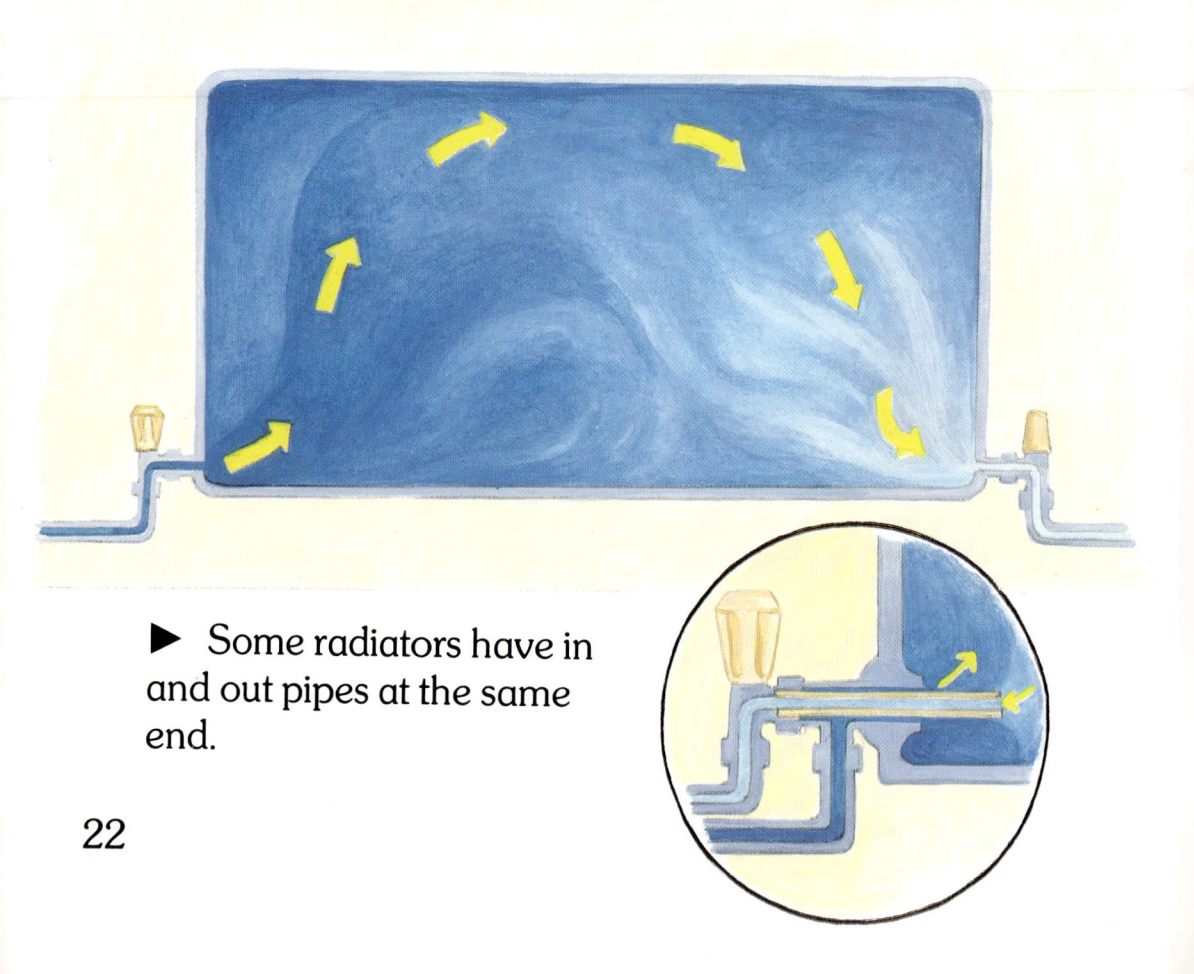

▶ Some radiators have in and out pipes at the same end.

Radiators Warming Up

1. Turn on a cold radiator. (Make sure the boiler is on.)

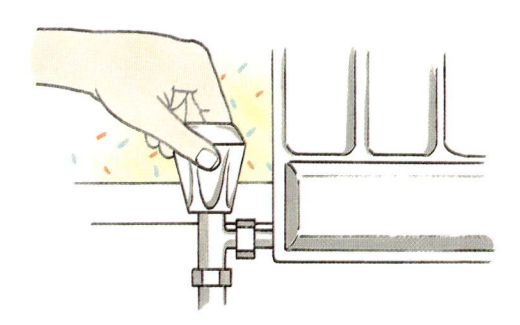

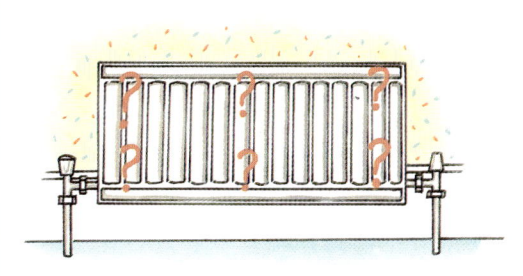

2. Can you guess which parts will warm up first?

3. Feel the hot water coming up the pipe and into the radiator.

4. Feel the radiator to work out where the hot water goes.

5. Draw the radiator and shade in the parts which warmed up first.

Metal and Heat

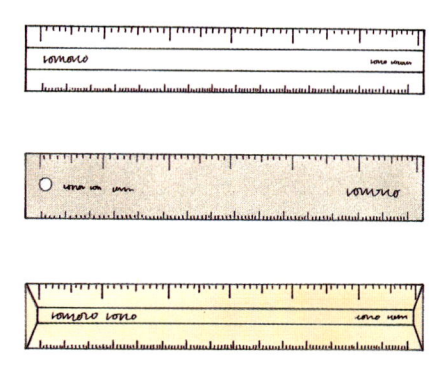

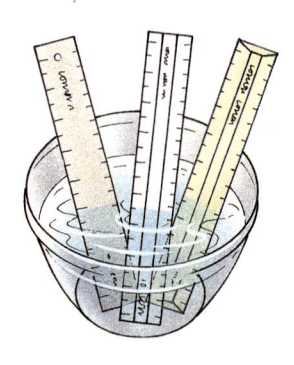

1. Find spoons or rulers made of metal, wood and plastic. Which feels warmest?

2. Dip them in a bowl filled with hot water for a few seconds.

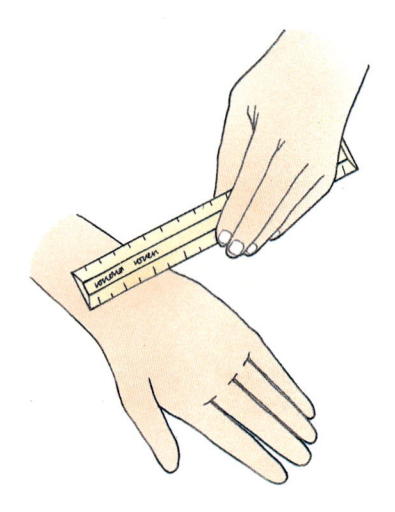

3. Wipe the water off quickly and feel the ends on your wrist. Which feels warmest now?

Count to fifty and feel them again.

Metal takes in heat quickly and lets it out quickly. This is why radiators are made of metal.

Heat from the water passes through the metal radiator. Heat rays travel out into the room.

The air around the radiator warms up. Warm air is lighter than cold air so the warm air floats upwards. This makes room for cooler air to get to the radiator.

You cannot see the air moving, but it swirls around and soon makes the whole room warm.

Warm Air Movements

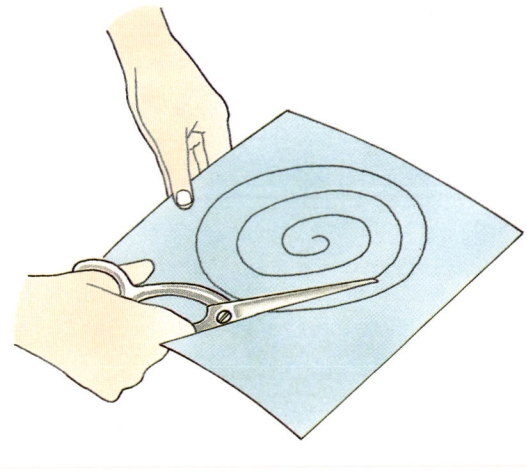

1. Draw a spiral on a circle of paper.

2. Cut along the line and thread cotton through the middle.

3. Hold or hang your spiral near a radiator or a heater and watch what happens.

4. The moving air pushes the spiral round.

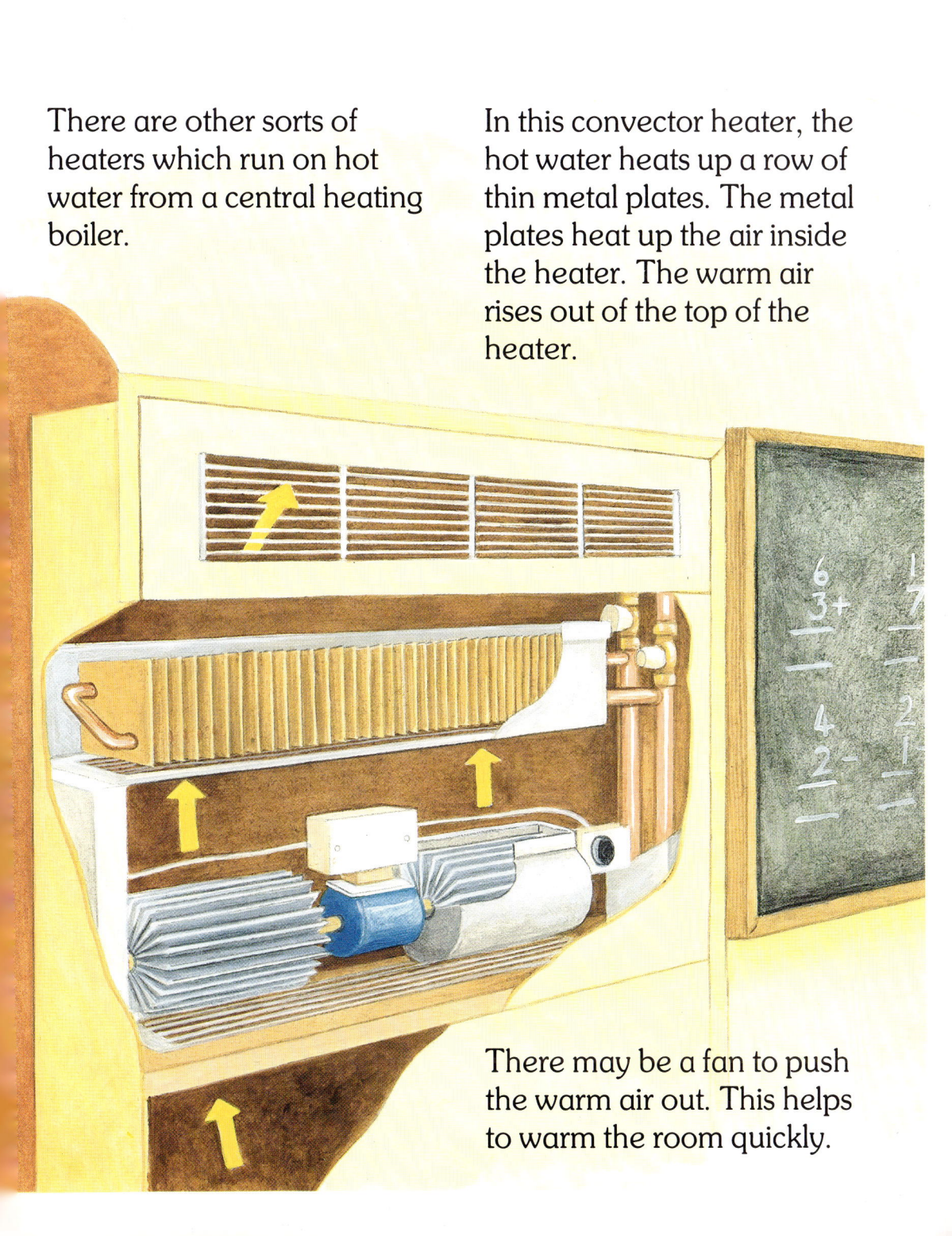

There are other sorts of heaters which run on hot water from a central heating boiler.

In this convector heater, the hot water heats up a row of thin metal plates. The metal plates heat up the air inside the heater. The warm air rises out of the top of the heater.

There may be a fan to push the warm air out. This helps to warm the room quickly.

Central heating can be controlled to give out the right amount of heat at the right times.

A clock near the boiler can be set to turn the heat on at the times it is needed.

A thermostat measures the temperature of the air. It turns the heating off if the temperature gets too high. It turns the heating on again if the temperature drops.

Rooms are usually heated to a temperature of around 20 degrees on the centigrade scale.

The air in a room cools down like the tea in a teapot.

Heat escapes through roofs and floors and walls and windows.

It is expensive to make heat. If the house is well-insulated the heat lasts longer.

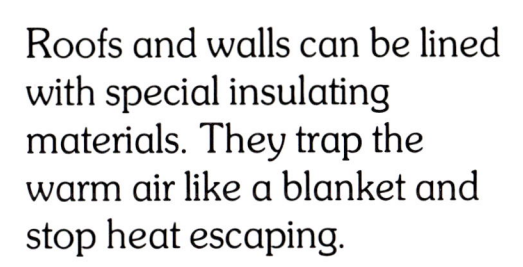

Roofs and walls can be lined with special insulating materials. They trap the warm air like a blanket and stop heat escaping.

Double-glazed windows also help to keep the heat in.

Insulation

1. Find two jam jars of the same size. Insulate one jar by wrapping it in a woollen cloth and fill both jars with hot water.

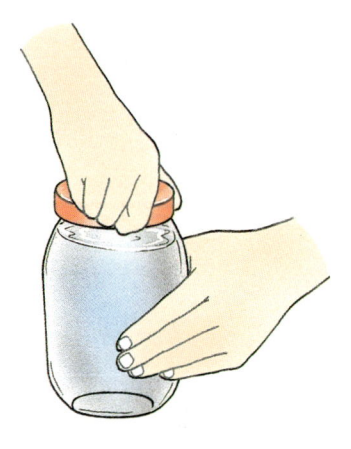

2. Screw the lids on lightly.

3. Put your hands around the jars. Can you feel heat escaping?

4. Each half hour, feel the warmth of the water in the jars, or measure the temperature with a thermometer.

How much longer does the water in the insulated jar stay warm?

In summer as the air outside warms up the air indoors warms up too.

All the heat we need comes from the biggest fire of all . . . the sun.

Index

boiler 16, 17, 18, 20, 21, 23, 28

centigrade scale 28
central heating 16–28
clock (central heating) 28
coal 7, 8
coils of wire 12, 13
convector heaters 13

danger 7
double-glazed windows 29

electric heaters 12–14
electricity 7, 12, 13, 14, 21
energy 10
expansion pipe 19

fan heater 13
fires 7, 8, 9, 10, 11, 16, 17, 31
flames 9, 11, 12, 16
fuel 11, 16

gas 7, 11, 16
   pipe 11

heat 11, 25, 29, 30, 31
   energy 10
   rays 10, 12, 25
heaters 7, 12
   convector 13
   electric 12–14
   fan 13
   storage 14, 15

heating 6
   central 16–28

insulation 29

metal 12, 16, 17, 22, 25

oil 7, 16
open fire 8
oxygen 8, 9

pilot light 16
pipes 8, 18, 19, 21, 22, 23
pump 21

radiators 7, 18, 20, 21, 22, 24, 25

storage heaters 14, 15

tanks 17, 19
temperature 28, 30
thermostat 28, 30

underfloor pipe 8

valve 22

water 21
   box 17
   cold 17
   hot 17, 18, 22, 23, 24, 30
white clay 11
wood 7, 8, 24